Phonics Stationery

by Marilyn Myers Burch

NEW YORK • TORONTO • LONDON • AUCKLAND • SYDNEY
MEXICO CITY • NEW DELHI • HONG KONG • BUENOS AIRES

SCHOLASTIC
Teaching
Resources

Special thanks to Betsy Yarbrough, Danielle Blood,
Maxie Chambliss, Jacqueline Swensen, and John Furlong
for their contributions to this book.

Cover design by Solas
Cover and interior illustrations by Maxie Chambliss
Interior design by Solutions by Design, Inc.
Edited by Betsy Yarbrough

ISBN: 0-439-51771-0

Contents

Phonics Stationery

Vowels

Blends

Digraphs

Introduction

Welcome to *Phonics Stationery*—a delightful way to make writing time extra special and help children build phonics skills! Each lined sheet of reproducible stationery is in the shape of an object or creature whose name includes the featured vowel, blend, or digraph. You'll find a unicorn for long *u*, a frog for short *o*, a clown, dragon, and snowman for blends, a phone and a shell for digraphs, and many more. The illustration provides a frame for students' writing and gives them an image to link to the sound. Below each image is a short word bank to provide additional examples of words that include the same sound and spark ideas for a variety of writing assignments. Emergent writers might expand the word bank and draw a small illustration for each word. More advanced writers might write short stories, poems, letters, or even tongue twisters! Additional ideas for using the stationery sheets in learning-rich activities appear in the next section.

How to Use This Book

The 25 stationery sheets in this book provide a variety of ways to enliven phonics study by helping children create personal links to written letters and their sounds. *Phonics Stationery* helps reinforce long and short vowels, as well as several consonant blends and digraphs. In this book, the term *blend* is used to describe both the spoken and written form of the letter clusters in which each consonant sound is heard. A digraph is a cluster of consonants that stand for one sound.

These pages are designed for flexible use. In addition to their primary function as stationery, they can also be used in many different lessons, games, and activities. Suggestions are provided below, but you and your students are bound to develop your own unique ways to put *Phonics Stationery* to use in your classroom.

Getting Started

Look through the table of contents to choose a stationery sheet for a particular vowel, blend, or digraph that you would like to reinforce, for example *st*. Before distributing the stationery sheets, introduce children to the format with a mini-lesson such as the one that follows for the *s*-blend *st*.

4

1. Write the letters *st* on chart paper. Ask if anyone can identify the letters and say the sounds they represent.

2. Below the letters, write the word *star* and draw a picture. Blend the word out loud, sweeping your finger beneath each letter. Ask a volunteer to come up and underline or highlight the letters *st* and say the sounds they represent.

3. Enlarge the *st* stationery sheet and display it. You might cover up or cut off the word bank for this step. Have the class brainstorm a list of words that begin with *st* as you record the words on the sheet.

4. Give each child a copy of the *st* stationery sheet. Challenge students to list words that begin with *st*. (You might have children list words that include rather than begin with the featured sound.) They can choose words from the class-generated list or choose other words. Have students draw a small illustration for some or all of the words.

5. Ask children to work with a partner and make up sentences about the words on their list. Challenge them to include as many words as they can in a single sentence. Encourage children to be imaginative and even a little silly as they think of ways to incorporate the words on the list into a few sentences. (It might be necessary to conduct a similar mini-lesson to introduce vowels and digraphs.)

6. When children are ready for more of a challenge, have them write sentences on their stationery sheet that include words with the featured sound. You might also have them write letters, poems, riddles, tongue twisters, or descriptions inspired by the illustration on the stationery sheet.

Imaginary Journeys

Create a list of real or imaginary locations to accompany the blends. For example, you might write Florida, Pleasantville, Snowflake Mountain, Starfish Cove, and Swan Lake. Or you might let students explore maps and globes to generate their own list. Next, tell students to put on their "walking shoes" and accompany you on a trip. Taking turns, describe what you "see" on your way to each location. You might start the class off by stating, "On our **fl**ight to **Fl**orida I saw a **fl**ag, but that's not what Sally saw. Let's hear what Sally saw." Sally would then repeat what you saw, describe a new **fl** sight, and call on someone else. She might say, "On our **fl**ight to **Fl**orida, Ms. Smith saw a **fl**ag and I saw a **fl**attened **fl**y, but that's not what James saw. Let's hear what James saw." Have a student come to the chalkboard and record the items that have been seen. When the class gets stumped for new words, change to a different blend and start again with students who have not yet had a turn.

Word Builders

Make a set of pink flashcards with a blend or digraph on each. Make another set of blue flashcards with a word family on each, such as:

-ick	-ag	-ight
-eck	-im	-ot
-ace	-ed	-in
-ip	-op	-ain

Let students work in pairs to create as many words as they can by combining one pink and one blue card. You might also have students create "new" words and give them original definitions. Ask volunteers to stand in front of the class and present the invented words with exaggerated movements. Have them place the beginning sound in one hand and the ending sound in the other. Instruct them to say each sound separately while holding up the appropriate card, and then to blend together the sounds.

Phonics Collage Posters

Display several large sheets of posterboard around the classroom. Attach a sheet of stationery to each sheet of posterboard. Distribute magazines to students and let them work alone or in pairs to find and cut out images whose names feature each displayed vowel, blend, or digraph. After allowing time to find some images, have students share what they have cut out. If an image fits with a displayed sound, invite the student to glue or tape the image to the appropriate poster and to write the name of the image beneath the picture.

Sound Circle

Make a copy of each stationery sheet and write the vowel, blend, or digraph in large, colorful letters in the center of the page (for example, long *a*). For this activity, you will also need a soft foam ball and a large open space. Select enough stationery sheets so that each child has one and place these sheets in a large circle on the floor. Ask children to select a sheet and stand or sit behind it. Toss the ball to a student. Explain that this student should say the sound(s) represented by the vowel, blend, or digraph in front of him or her. For a greater challenge, have students say one or more words that begin with or include this sound. Once a player completes a turn, the player tosses the ball to someone who has not yet had a turn.

Stationery for Any Occasion

Before you begin using the stationery, look through the illustrations to get ideas for additional ways to use the sheets. You might use the stationery to connect to other lessons. For example, you might use the long *e* stationery (tree) for a unit on trees or as part of a seasonal study. The *sn* stationery of a snowman works well for winter, short *a* (basket) for spring, and long *o* (boat) and digraph *sh* (shell) for summer. You might also tie the stationery into children's experiences at school. For example, children could write about their experience in a school performance on the *s*-blend sheet of a stage. Or you could compile all of the animal images to form a phonics zoo. Have fun as you find ways to use the stationery in ways that best meet the needs of your students.

Here are other high-utility vowel, blend, and digraph lists you may want to review with your class:

Long a	Long e	Long i	Long o	Long u
face	beach	bike	bone	argue
grape	feet	dime	cold	cube
maze	green	fire	go	fuse
place	leap	hide	joke	future
same	mean	kite	old	January
take	peek	light	pillow	menu
tale	sheep	mice	shadow	mule
wave	teach	wife	toad	pupil

Short a	Short e	Short i	Short o	Short u
cat	bed	big	box	bump
crack	chest	dip	clock	cup
grab	dress	fish	doll	dunk
hat	egg	gill	fog	fuss
match	nest	kiss	hot	hug
pal	peck	six	pot	luck
splash	sell	slip	soft	suds
stamp	wet	swim	stop	up

l-blends

cl	pl
clam	plan
class	plane
clear	planet
cling	pleasant
cloud	plug

fl
flame
flat
flight
flood
floss

r-blends

br	dr
brave	drew
bread	drift
brick	drink
broom	drop
brush	dry

cr	tr
crab	trash
creek	tree
crib	trip
cross	truck
crowd	trust

s-blends

sk	sp	sw
sketch	spark	swap
skid	spell	sweep
skill	spoon	swell
skin	sport	swing
skit	spout	swoop

sn	st
snail	stack
snake	stay
snap	steep
sneak	stir
snow	story

Digraphs

ch	ph	sh
chair	dolphin	shake
change	pharmacy	shape
chart	photocopy	shark
cherry	Ralph	show
chill	trophy	ship

VOWEL
Long a

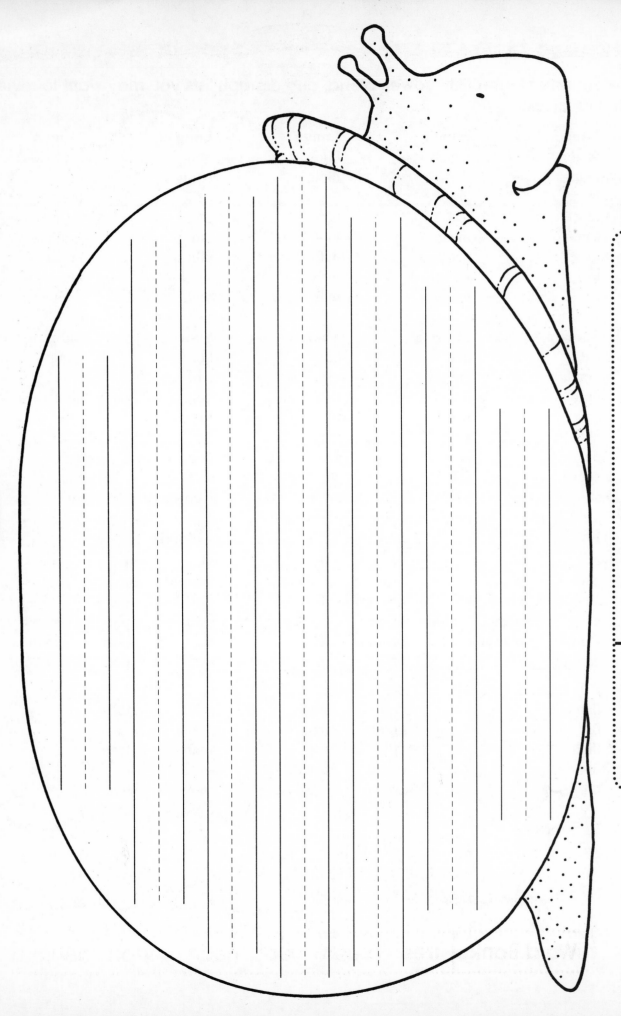

Word Bank | snail day lake name play rain

Phonics Stationery Scholastic Teaching Resources

Word Bank | **tree** dream leaf near queen sleep

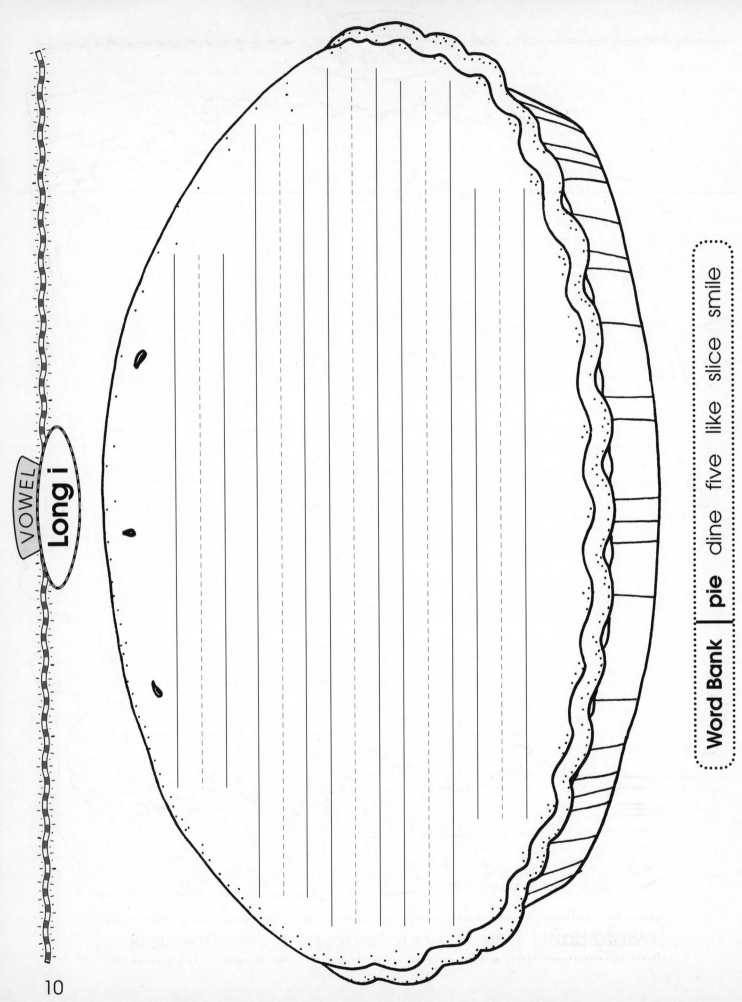

VOWEL

Long i

Word Bank | **pie** dine five like slice smile

Phonics Stationery Scholastic Teaching Resources

Word Bank | **boat** coast coat float rode row

VOWEL

Long u

Word Bank | unicorn bugle cute huge music use

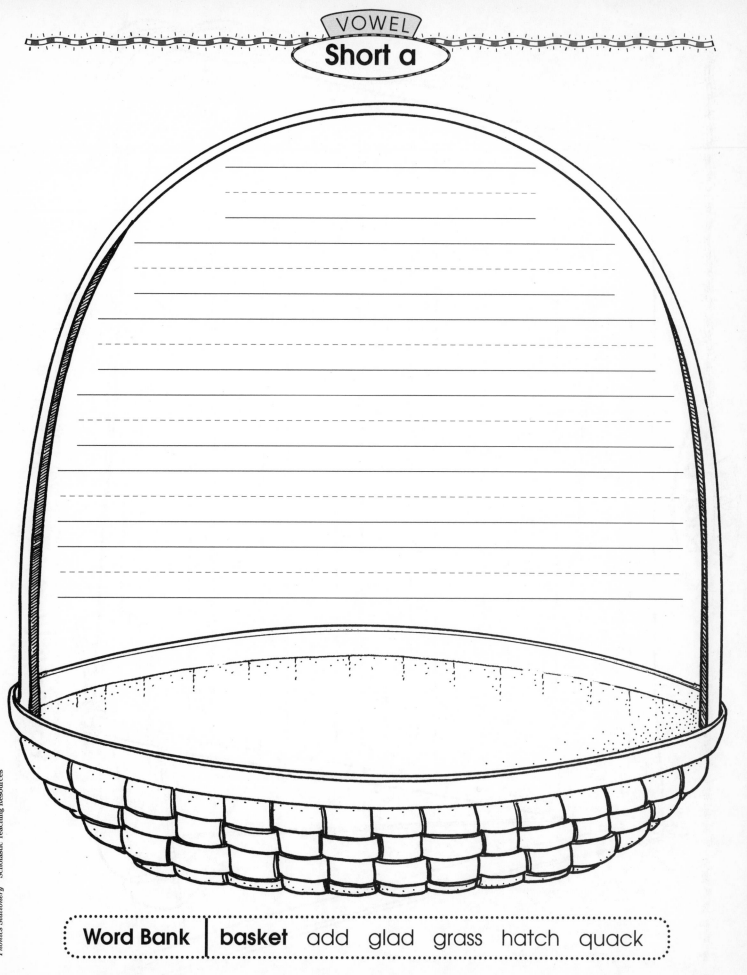

Word Bank | **basket** add glad grass hatch quack

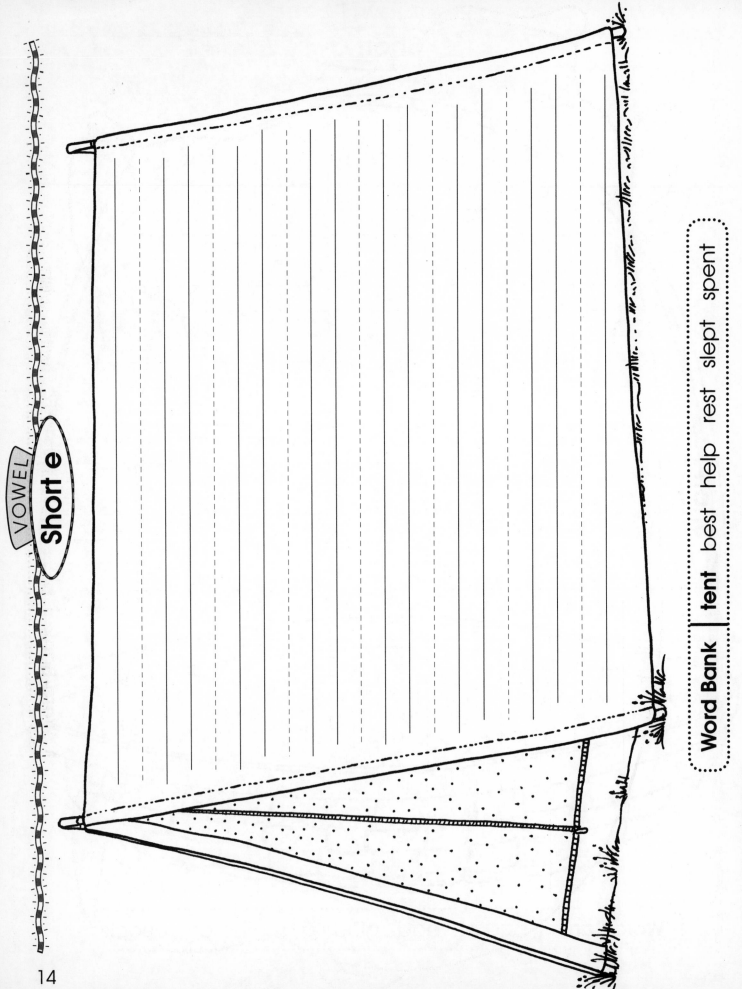

VOWEL

Short e

Word Bank | tent best help rest slept spent

Phonics Stationery   Scholastic Teaching Resources

VOWEL

Short i

Word Bank | **pig** brick hill mix twig wish

Phonics Stationery Scholastic Teaching Resources

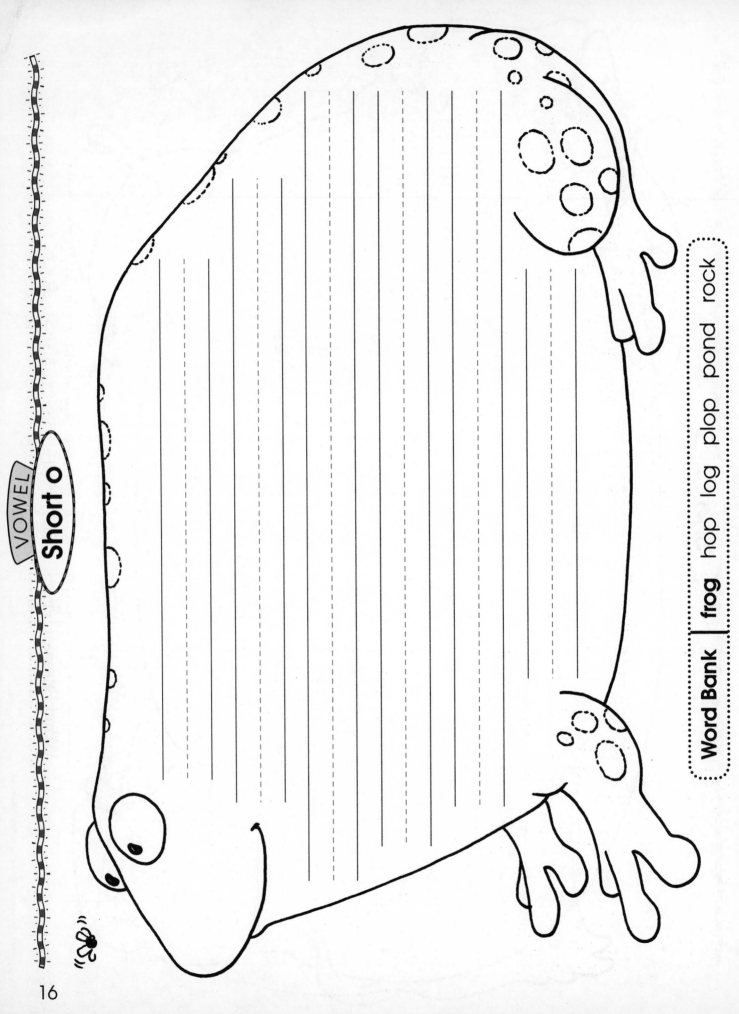

VOWEL

Short o

Word Bank | frog hop log plop pond rock

VOWEL

Short u

Word Bank | **duck** bug fun mud stuck tug

Phonics Stationery Scholastic Teaching Resources

Word Bank | **clown** clap clever climb clothes clue

Phonics Stationery Scholastic Teaching Resources

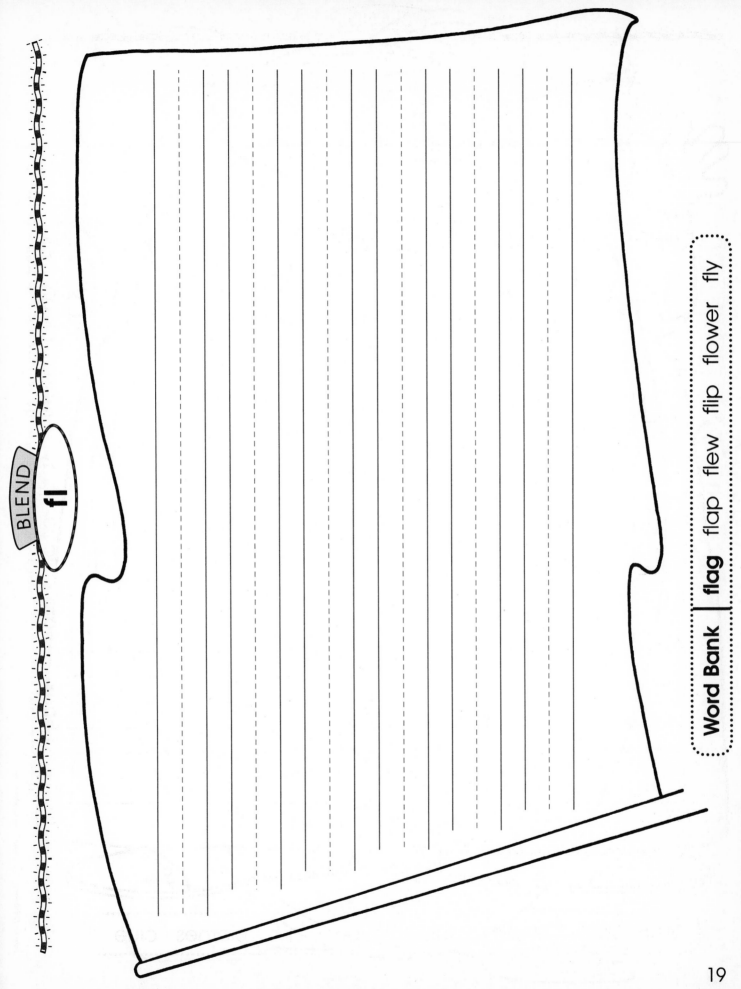

BLEND

fl

Word Bank | **flag** flap flew flip flower fly

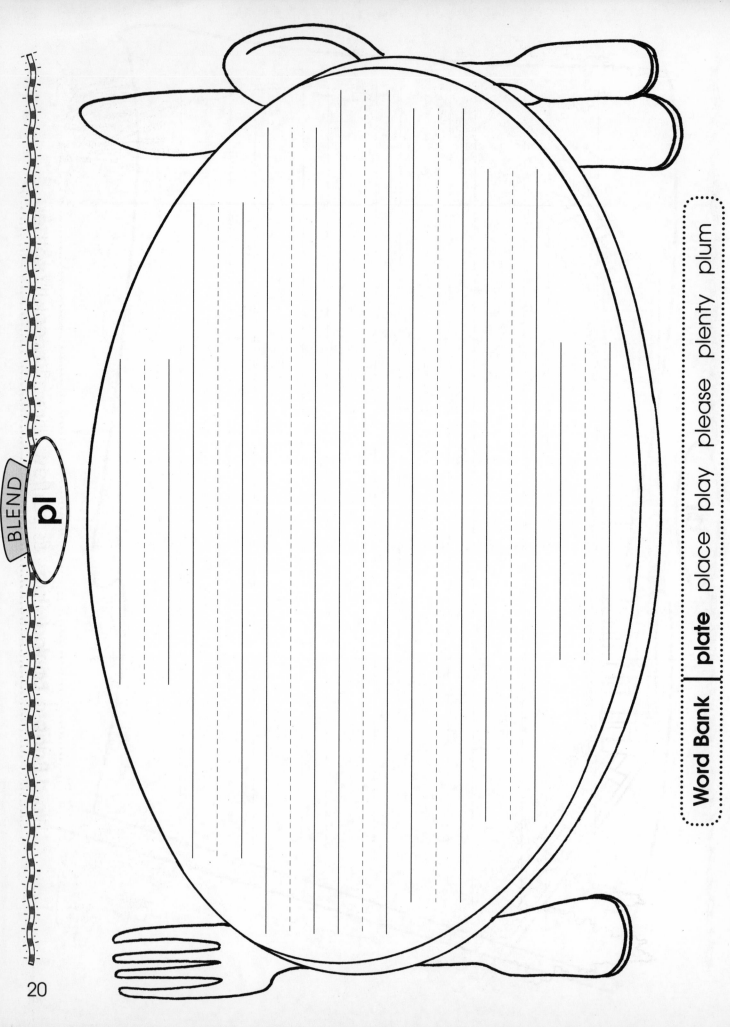

BLEND

pl

Word Bank | **plate** place play please plenty plum

Phonics Stationery Scholastic Teaching Resources

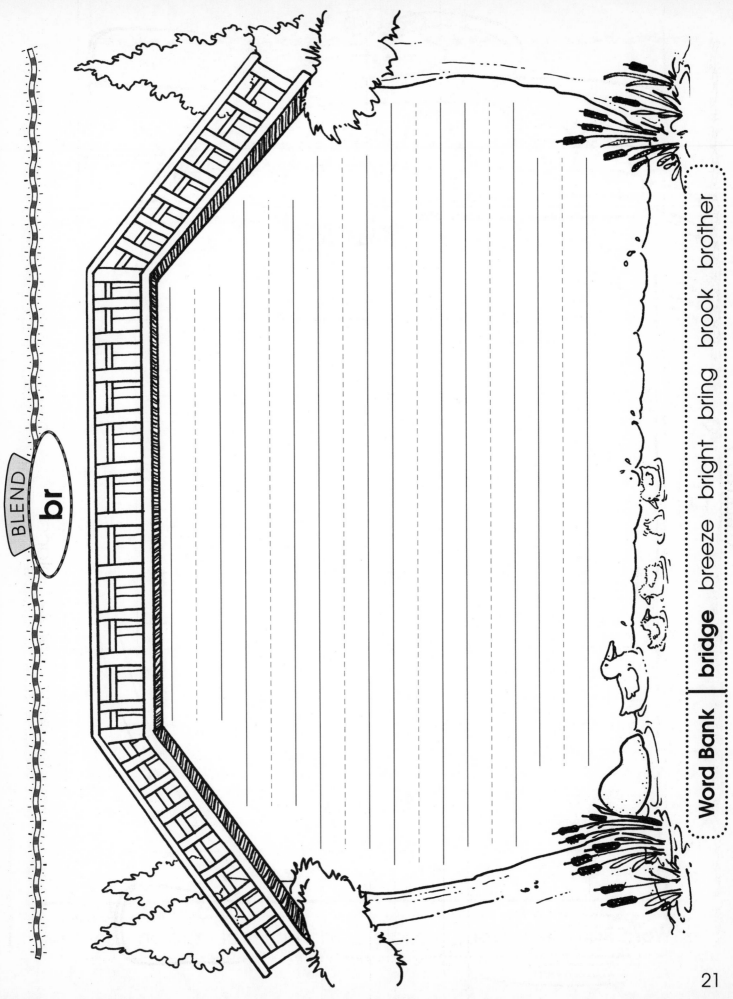

BLEND

br

Word Bank | **bridge** breeze bright bring brook brother

Word Bank | **crayons** cradle craft cricket crown cry

Phonics Stationery Scholastic Teaching Resources

dr

Word Bank | **dragon** draw dream dress drive drum

Phonics Stationery Scholastic Teaching Resources

Word Bank | **trophy** trade travel treasure true try

Phonics Stationery Scholastic Teaching Resources

Word Bank | **skunk** skate ski skip skirt sky

Phonics Stationery Scholastic Teaching Resources

Word Bank | **snowman** snack sneeze sniff snore snug

Phonics Stationery Scholastic Teaching Resources

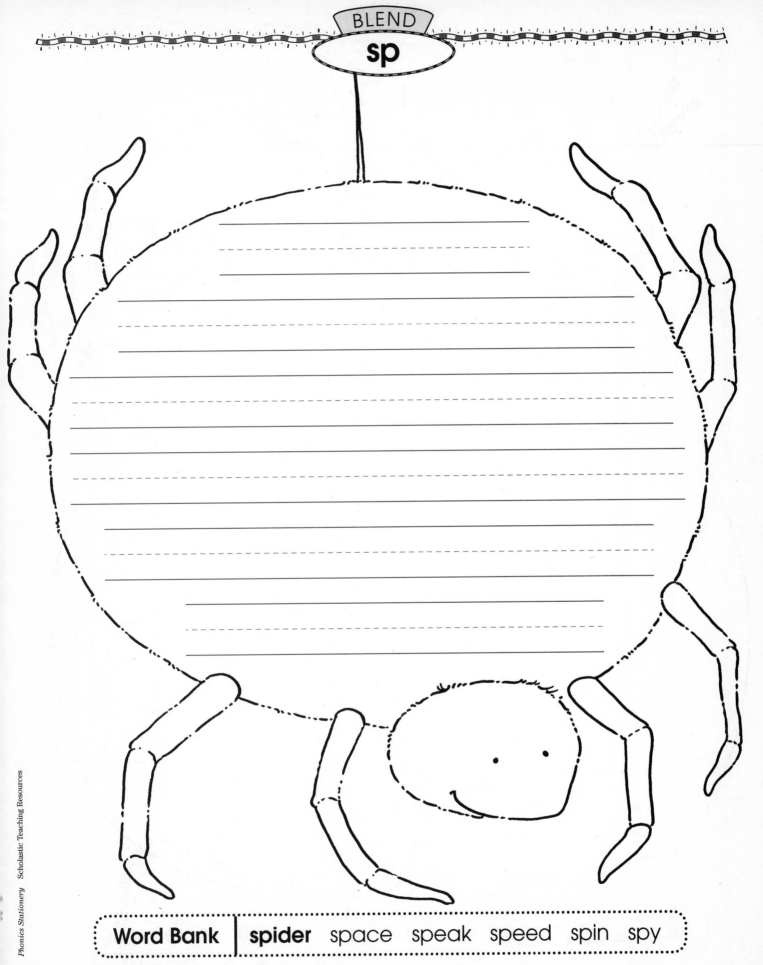

Word Bank | **spider** space speak speed spin spy

Phonics Stationery Scholastic Teaching Resources

BLEND

st

Word Bank | **stage** stand star stomach stop student

Word Bank | swan swamp sway sweet swiftly swim

Word Bank | **cheese** chase cheer chew chicken chunk

Phonics Stationery Scholastic Teaching Resources

Word Bank | **phone** alphabet elephant graph nephew photo

sh

Word Bank shell shallow sharp shiny shout shovel